The Era of Digital Gold for Entrepreneurs

Utilizing your enterprise to build wealth with Bitcoin

Steve T. Lynch

All rights reserved. No part of this publication may be reproduced, distributed, or transmitted in any form or by any means, including photocopying, recording, or other electronic or mechanical methods, without the prior written permission of the publisher, except in the case of brief quotations embodied in critical reviews and certain other noncommercial uses permitted by copyright law.

Copyright © **Steve T. Lynch,** 2024

TABLE OF CONTENT

PART 1	**5**
UNDERSTANDING BITCOIN	**5**
CHAPTER 1	**6**
How Bitcoin Started	6
CHAPTER 2	**13**
Why is Bitcoin Important?	13
CHAPTER 3	**21**
How To Buy Bitcoin	21
CHAPTER 4	**27**
How To Use Bitcoin	27
PART 2	**34**
BECOMING A BITCOIN ENTREPRENEUR	**34**
CHAPTER 5	**35**
Bitcoin Risks and Opportunities	35
CHAPTER 6	**42**
How to Make Money With Bitcoin	42
CHAPTER 7	**53**
Why Should Entrepreneurs Care About Bitcoin?	53
Part 3	**68**
GETTING STARTED INVESTING IN BITCOIN	**68**
CHAPTER 8	**69**
How to invest in Bitcoin wisely	69
CHAPTER 9	**77**
Best Bitcoin Trading Strategies	77
CHAPTER 10	**84**
Bitcoin and Entrepreneurship	84
Conclusion	**89**

PART 1

UNDERSTANDING BITCOIN

CHAPTER 1

How Bitcoin Started

The cryptography mailing group at the metzdowd website received an announcement from Nakamoto in October 2008: "I've been working on a new electronic cash system that's fully peer-to-peer, with no trusted third party." "Bitcoin: A Peer-to-Peer Electronic Cash System," a now-famous white paper posted on the Bitcoin website, would serve as the foundation for modern Bitcoin operations.

The first decentralized cryptocurrency is called Bitcoin (abbreviation: BTC; sign: ₿). Bitcoin was created in 2008 by an unidentified individual named **Satoshi Nakamoto** and is based on the free-market philosophy. Since its open-source implementation was released in 2009, bitcoin has been used as money. El Salvador made it legal tender in 2021. Most people see it as an investment, and some academics have called it an economic bubble. Due to its pseudonymous nature, the use of Bitcoin by criminals has drawn the attention of authorities, and as a result, some nations have banned it as of 2021.

Without centralized control, nodes in the peer-to-peer Bitcoin network use encryption to validate transactions and log them in a publicly accessible distributed ledger known as a blockchain. Mining, a computationally demanding process based on proof of work, is used to protect the Bitcoin blockchain by achieving consensus across nodes. Mining has been condemned for its negative effects on the environment and for using a lot of power.

Block One

The first Bitcoin block was mined on January 3, 2009. Perhaps evidence that the block was mined on or after that date can be found in the line "The Times 03/Jan/2009 Chancellor on the brink of second bailout for banks," often referred to as Block 0, or the genesis block.

Incentives

Every two hundred thousand blocks, Bitcoin payouts are cut in half. In 2009, for instance, the block reward was fifty new bitcoins. The third halving, which took place on May 11, 2020, reduced the reward for each block to 6.25 bitcoins. The prize was reduced to 3.125 bitcoins at the fourth halving, which took place in April

2024. The reward will drop to 1.5625 BTC at the next halving, which is anticipated to occur in mid-2028.

Denominations

One bitcoin is divisible to eight decimal places (100 millionths of one bitcoin), and this smallest unit is referred to as a satoshi.

The Blockchain Technology of Bitcoin

The digital currency known as Bitcoin is easy to comprehend. For instance, you can send smaller amounts of your Bitcoin as payment for goods or services using your cryptocurrency wallet. Bitcoin, on the other hand, operates in a very complicated manner.

The blockchain

A distributed ledger, or blockchain, is a shared database of data connected by cryptographic methods. "Distributed" refers to the fact that, unlike most data storage, it is kept on several computers rather than a single server location.

These computers are equipped with a network of automated programs that manage the blockchain and carry out the tasks required for it to function.

On a blockchain, a block is a file that includes the transactions that were recorded in the block, the transaction counter, and the block header. The block header is composed of multiple elements, whereas the transaction counter lists the transactions in the block:

- Software version: The version of the blockchain that is currently operating (also known as the magic number)
- previous block hash: The data from the previous block that was encrypted

- Merkle root: All of the hashed data from earlier transactions is contained in a single hash (encrypted information).
- Timestamp: The time and date that the block was opened is known as the timestamp.
- Difficulty target: The current network difficulty problem miners are attempting to solve for
- Nonce: Short for "number used once," which is used to solve the mining problem and open the block.

As noted, each block contains the hashed information of the previous block. This creates a chain of encrypted blocks (files) that contain information from all previous blocks, going back to the first block of the blockchain.

Encryption

Bitcoin uses the SHA-256 hashing algorithm to encrypt (hash) the data stored in the blocks on the blockchain. Simply put, transaction data stored in a block is encrypted into a 256-bit (64-digit) hexadecimal number. That number contains all the transaction data and information linked to the blocks before that block.

CHAPTER 2

Why is Bitcoin Important?

Bitcoin has been lauded as an innovation that has the potential to revolutionize the world.

For almost 25 years, cryptographers and inventors have been attempting to come up with a safe and decentralized functional digital currency, but none succeeded until the birth of Bitcoin.

So what makes Bitcoin different? And why is it such a game-changer?

In this essay, we highlight the important arguments.

Bitcoin is permissionless

With the exception of paper currency (something that is becoming uncommon as the world continues to become digital), conventional currencies need authorization to use. This implies that third parties like banks, financial organizations, and governments stand between you and your money.

Bitcoin needs no permission from anybody. It is free and accessible to use internationally. There are no boundaries or restrictions with Bitcoin.

Bitcoin is impervious to seizure

Since it is not stored at any central bank or firm, Nobody can confiscate your Bitcoin*. With Bitcoin, you can be your own bank.

*Note that this is only true if you keep your Bitcoin in self-custody using a program like the Bitcoin.com Wallet app.

Bitcoin is censorship resistant

Censorship resistance in Bitcoin refers to its capacity to allow transactions that can't be banned, changed, or reversed by any government, organization, or person. This is feasible due to Bitcoin's decentralized structure and blockchain technology. The Bitcoin system runs on cryptographic principles guaranteeing that once a transaction is validated, it cannot be changed or destroyed.

Bitcoin is decentralized

The Bitcoin network is dispersed internationally across many thousands of nodes (computers) and millions of users, where you don't have to depend on trustworthy third parties. The decentralized structure of Bitcoin also makes it particularly anti-fragile. In other words, it's nearly impossible to destroy the Bitcoin network.

Bitcoin has a limited quantity

There will only ever be 21 million bitcoins produced, and they're generated at a predictable pace over the next 100 years. This makes Bitcoin a rare commodity, which is a significant part of why it is valued. By contrast, fiat currencies like the dollar have a limitless supply. While the buying power of the dollar falls year after year, the value of Bitcoin continues to climb.

Bitcoin is open source

The Bitcoin protocol (software) is accessible for anybody to view. Additionally, anybody may contribute to improving Bitcoin. This implies that the way Bitcoin develops over time is completely up to the Bitcoin community, which is defined as anybody who has Bitcoin or has an interest in its future. Bitcoin is the people's money.

Bitcoin gives privacy

If handled appropriately, Bitcoin may be used as an anonymous money free from snooping governments. When you use Bitcoin, you don't need to submit your email, name, social security number, or any other identifying information. Bitcoin is merely numbers, 1's and 0's, going via the internet.

Bitcoin supports democracy

Because Bitcoin is anonymous, individuals all around the globe use it to fight back against oppression. When authoritarian countries shut off the bank accounts of dissidents, Bitcoin may still be used to pay rallies and assist freedom fighters.

Bitcoin is a push mechanism

With Bitcoin, there is no possibility of chargebacks since once Bitcoin is transferred, the transaction cannot be reversed. Bitcoin is analogous to currency -- once you give someone cash, you cannot get it back (currency—onceunless they give it back to you).

Bitcoin is real money

Bitcoin is utilized across the globe to pay for products such as coffee, food, gadgets, travel, and more. Some even prefer to call it magical internet money because of all its great features, including its capacity to not be double-spent.

All you need is an internet connection to use Bitcoin

You can purchase and trade Bitcoin from your phone or computer. You can even use it to pay for things directly from your Bitcoin wallet in establishments that accept it as a form of payment. Moreover, those who can't access conventional banking systems may make use of Bitcoin instead—as long as they have a gadget that can connect to the internet. More recently, bitcoin credit cards have become available, meaning you don't even need the internet to spend your Bitcoin.

Bitcoin is transparent

All information regarding the Bitcoin money supply is available for anyone to view on the blockchain. Every transaction done with Bitcoin is open for anybody to view too, however personal information is masked. This unprecedented transparency helps guarantee that Bitcoin stays open and free from corruption.

Bitcoin is freedom

Using Bitcoin gives you the financial freedom to transact globally using all the properties mentioned above. As such, Bitcoin provides economic stability and newfound freedoms to the world, making it a truly game-changing technology.

CHAPTER 3

How To Buy Bitcoin

You may purchase Bitcoin via a cryptocurrency exchange if you don't want to mine it. Due to its high price, most individuals will not be able to buy a whole Bitcoin, but you may buy parts of it on these exchanges using fiat money like US dollars.

More than ever, Bitcoin has been booming. The original cryptocurrency got within a few hundred dollars of $100,000 on Friday, reaching another all-time high, which would have been unthinkable ten years ago or even in early 2023 when Bitcoin was trading closer to $20,000, despite a little decline over the weekend.

Bulls anticipate that the trend will continue, and many believe that before the year is out, Bitcoin will reach the six-figure milestone.

When Bitcoin was first developed, mining it yourself was the only method to get it. Nowadays, investors may purchase it in a variety of ways, giving them complete control over their money.

Here is a guide to the three most sensible methods to purchase Bitcoin if you want to join in on the excitement but are unsure how.

Exchanges for Cryptocurrencies

Using an exchange is one of the simplest methods to buy Bitcoin; the largest and finest exchanges are similar to using a standard online bank or brokerage.

Platform-specific transaction fees are how exchanges generate revenue. Customers may purchase Bitcoin using fiat money or other digital assets, and the exchange will safely store your cryptocurrency in addition to collecting a fee from each transaction.

It's crucial to remember that not every cryptocurrency exchange is reliable. Some exchanges, like the notorious FTX, have failed as a result of dubious business practices and poor money management.

Coinbase, Robinhood, and Kraken are well-known cryptocurrency exchanges in the United States. Following fulfillment of know-your-customer criteria, such as presenting a legitimate ID, users may download the app to their phone, create an account, and begin trading.

Exchange-traded funds

Investing in Bitcoin via an exchange-traded fund is an additional option. Investors may get exposure to an underlying asset via exchange-traded funds (ETFs) without actually owning that asset. Customers may purchase shares in a variety of Bitcoin ETFs from well-known brokerages, including Schwab and Fidelity.

In January, the Securities and Exchange Commission authorized spot Bitcoin ETFs, which made it possible for conventional financial institutions to provide Bitcoin investment for the first time. These businesses keep a careful eye on the price of Bitcoin as it changes and store it in addition to offering investors shares.

Investors who don't want to handle the hassles of direct Bitcoin ownership may find these funds helpful. An ETF provides a simple method to increase your exposure to the asset if you already have a portfolio of investments. The largest Bitcoin ETFs are Ark Invest's ARKB, Fidelity's FBTC, and BlackRock's IBIT.

Self-Custody Wallets

Using a self-custody wallet might be the best option if you desire complete control over your digital assets. These wallets generate and save your private and public keys, communicate with the blockchain, and enable you to freely move your assets and keep an eye on your balance.

A self-custody wallet's drawback is that you are in charge of keeping your private data safe. Similar to a password, your private key gives anybody access to the money in your wallet. Finding a secure location to keep your private key is crucial since, unlike a password, if you lose it, there is no way to get it back and your digital assets are probably gone forever.

You may download the majority of self-custody wallets on your phone. The DeFi wallet from Crypto.com, Metamask, and Coinbase Wallet are well-known examples.

CHAPTER 4

How To Use Bitcoin

When Bitcoin was first created and made available, it was a peer-to-peer payment system. However, because of its rising value, competition from other blockchains and cryptocurrencies, and advancements on blockchains that process data for the Bitcoin blockchain, its use cases are expanding.

Use for payments

As of 2018, bitcoin is often used to buy illicit products online, although it is seldom utilized in transactions with businesses. Typically, exchanges include conversions into fiat currency, and prices are not stated in Bitcoin. Significant prices, the inability to handle chargebacks, significant price volatility, lengthy transaction times, and transaction fees (particularly for minor transactions) are often mentioned reasons for not utilizing Bitcoin. According to Bloomberg, bitcoin is being used for cross-border payments to freelancers and for large-item sales on the website Overstock.com. Despite the hefty costs levied by banks and Western Union, competitors in this sector, there was minimal evidence of bitcoin usage in international remittances as of 2015. In 2022, it was noted that the restaurant industry was using bitcoin more and more in addition to cash and credit cards, despite the dangers and expenses involved.

The Bitcoin Law made bitcoin and the US dollar legal money in El Salvador in September 2021. Both domestically and internationally, the adoption has drawn criticism. The International Monetary Fund (IMF) called on El Salvador to change its mind in 2022. Bitcoin use in El Salvador is still somewhat low as of 2022, with 80% of companies refusing to take it. Together with the CFA franc, bitcoin was made legal in the Central African Republic (CAR) in April 2022, but the change was revoked a year later.

Some countries also utilize Bitcoin. For example, after originally opposing cryptocurrencies, the Iranian government now views them as a way to get over sanctions. In order to utilize Bitcoin for imports, Iran has mandated from 2020 that local bitcoin miners sell their cryptocurrency to the Central Bank of Iran. A few member states, such as Zug (Switzerland) and Colorado (US), also accept bitcoin as payment for taxes. The US government has roughly $5 billion worth of confiscated bitcoin as of 2023.

Many businesses, stores, and merchants accept Bitcoin as payment for products and services.

Cryptocurrency-accepting physical businesses will often post a sign that reads, "Bitcoin Accepted Here." The necessary hardware terminal or wallet address may be used to manage the transactions using touchscreen applications and QR codes. By including Bitcoin as a payment option alongside credit cards, PayPal, and other online payment methods, an online company may easily take bitcoin.

You must have a cryptocurrency wallet in order to utilize your bitcoin. The private keys to your bitcoins may be stored in wallets, which serve as your blockchain interface. When you are doing a transaction, you have to input these keys.

Use for investment and status as an economic bubble

As Bitcoin gained prominence, it attracted the attention of investors and speculators. Cryptocurrency exchanges that made it easier to buy and sell Bitcoin appeared between 2009 and 2017. Demand gradually increased as prices started to climb, and in 2017 it surpassed $1,000 in price.

Many investors started purchasing Bitcoin as a long-term investment because they thought its price would continue to rise. The market took off when traders started making short-term deals on bitcoin exchanges.

The price of Bitcoin plummeted in 2022 after peaking at over $69,000 in November 2021. It reached a peak of $47,454 in March 2022, but by November, it had dropped to $15,731. After that, it bounced up in 2023, peaking at $31,474 before falling back below $30,000.

Because Bitcoin is viewed similarly to other assets by investors, its price tends to follow stock market patterns. The price fluctuations of Bitcoin, however, are wildly inflated and sometimes subject to thousands of dollar swings. Numerous Bitcoin investors have a tendency to "trade the news," as seen by the price swings that follow every noteworthy news occurrence.

As anticipation for the approval of Bitcoin Spot ETFs increased, the price of Bitcoin surged into the mid-$40,000s in early 2024. Following the approval of the ETFs, the price of Bitcoin surged to over $50,000 by the middle of February 2024.

PART 2

BECOMING A BITCOIN ENTREPRENEUR

CHAPTER 5

Bitcoin Risks and Opportunities

Bitcoin and crypto assets are a controversial issue. For believers, digital currencies represent the future of money, while to others they are anathema, make-believe commodities created on thin air. The reality probably falls somewhere in between. But in the end, the success of any cryptocurrency or token boils down to whether it has a future utility—and that comes with a hefty dollop of uncertainty.

Here's an analogy that sums it up. It would be prudent for me to purchase laundry tokens in advance of their price increase if I knew that in six months the cost of these tokens would double, and I needed to carry my laundry to the launderette every week for the following year. Laundry is the use case, and I can use the tokens to do laundry anytime I want. My laundry tokens will be useless if I do this and then purchase a washing machine. If everyone I know also has a washing machine, I could have a hard time selling them. And if the launderette shuts, making washing there impossible, I'd be left with a load of useless tokens.

This line of thinking may be extended to portions of the cryptocurrency market that stand for initiatives with unproven applications. There's a slim possibility that some will become "closed launderettes," even if there's a larger possibility that others may find practical uses and achieve broad acceptance. Due to the lack of regulation in the industry, it attracts unscrupulous individuals and even criminals.

thus, some tokens have proven to be complete frauds.

Even Bitcoin, the granddaddy of crypto, has problems that make it, in our opinion, unreliable as a store of value or an asset that generates a return. It doesn't constitute a claim on anything, and the use cases might be replaced by anything else. There is no value behind it, but for the energy used in its 'mining.' There is no cashflow, and there is neither interest nor dividend. To purchase it is an act of faith that others would attach a greater price to it in the future, which is far from certain when there is no inherent worth.

With no anchor of an asset to support it or income to guide its direction, the Bitcoin price sails on a wild sea of speculative activity, governed by the prevailing balance of FOMO and uncertainty. Presently it has wind in its sails owing to a predicted friendlier regulatory climate surrounding crypto when Donald Trump enters office next year. But it remains uncontrolled and very volatile, which means there might be sudden and large adjustments at any moment.

Reasons to be skeptical of Bitcoin and crypto

1. Volatility
Bitcoin and other cryptocurrencies are generally unregulated and display erratic price movements due to the absence of fundamentals underlying them. Gamblers may make enormous profits but can suffer terrible loses when emotion goes bad. In general, asset classes must produce a systematic return over time and/or provide a

secure store of value. The volatility of Bitcoin and its lack of physical value imply it do not fit any of these characteristics and so defy any logical examination.

2. Regulation

The current spike in the price of Bitcoin and other cryptocurrencies has come about due of US President-elect Donald Trump's positive statements on the issue. Having earlier expressed pessimism, Trump recently remarked, "If crypto is going to define the future, I want it to be mined, minted and made in the USA." He has also threatened to dismiss the current head of the Securities and Exchange Commission (SEC), Gary Gesler, who has clamped down on crypto throughout his term.

However, a Trump U-turn is not without precedent, and the recent frenzy may swiftly reverse if he changes his tune. Trump may begin to advocate deregulation of crypto in the form of stable currencies tied to and backed by the US rather than a competitive, closed currency such as Bitcoin or others. Ultimately, the new may be overtaken by the old in a different form.

3. A waste of energy

Mining Bitcoin is energy demanding since it requires computers competing to solve incredibly complicated challenges. That's by design. The effort and electricity that go into the mining process is what give the currency value, and many other cryptocurrencies employ similar 'proof of work' techniques. However, the large energy usage produces an inefficient and wasteful system at a time when energy supply is tight.

CHAPTER 6

How to Make Money With Bitcoin

Bitcoin, the biggest cryptocurrency by market cap, has had an unbelievable year. Bitcoin's price reached $100,000 for the first time on Dec. 4, 2024, a long-awaited milestone and is currently approaching another all-time high of $150,000 in 2025.

This milestone follows a succession of record highs after the November 2024 presidential election. Investors commonly assume that Donald Trump will be a pro-cryptocurrency (and anti-regulation) president.

Making money using Bitcoin (BTC) has grown more challenging. Prices are variable. Promises of free Bitcoin are typically frauds. Bitcoin mining, previously accessible to private investors, is now so competitive that it's seldom a successful endeavor for individuals with tiny setups.

However, it's still feasible to earn money using Bitcoin. You may sell it, lend it, retain it or earn it. Returns aren't guaranteed on this volatile asset; just as you may gain money when the price goes up, it's also conceivable you might lose money if the price goes down.

Holding Bitcoin

Return: Depends on the magnitude of investment and price fluctuations.

As an entrepreneur, buying and keeping Bitcoin as a long-term investment—or, as some crypto aficionados call it, HODLing—it may be a low-effort strategy to earn money in the long run, as long as its price when you ultimately sell it is greater than the price at which you got it.

Bitcoin was initially created as a cryptocurrency that could be used for day-to-day transactions, but as its value climbed, many investors have come to regard Bitcoin as a long-term investment. As with any investment, holding for a longer amount of time implies you'll have to tolerate ups and downs in price without being tempted to purchase or sell. If you want to purchase and keep Bitcoin, you'll want to make sure you're not overexposed to any one asset and that you're not investing money you can't afford to lose. One piece of advice is to invest no more than 10% of your portfolio into hazardous assets like Bitcoin.

How about Bitcoin ETFs?

In January 2024, the Securities and Exchange Commission authorized a number of spot Bitcoin ETFs. These enable investors—even 401(k) investors, who were previously unable to directly access Bitcoin via their retirement accounts—to obtain exposure to the cryptocurrency.

On the one hand, Bitcoin ETFs offer a convenient option for fund-oriented investors, such as those with retirement accounts, to dedicate a part of their portfolio to cryptocurrencies for the purpose of investing diversification. On the contrary, they lack many of the perks of genuine bitcoin ownership—you can't spend them or keep them in a cold wallet. And they may be prone to just as much volatility as Bitcoin itself.

Using a credit card with Bitcoin incentives

Return: Generally 3% or less per dollar spent on selected categories and 1% on all other purchases.

There are a few crypto credit cards that will enable you to earn rewards in Bitcoin. Similar to standard cash-back schemes, you may earn a tiny percentage of the purchases you make with the card, which can be paid out in Bitcoin or other cryptocurrencies. Some provide sign-up incentives that enable you to earn extra benefits if you satisfy specific conditions.

Keep in mind that your coin earnings can be decreased by transaction fees or a spread introduced by the supplier. A spread is the difference between the market price and the rate supplied by a specific platform; when the issuer of a crypto credit card has one that applies to rewards, it implies you'll obtain a somewhat less favorable exchange rate when both earning and selling those crypto rewards.

Lending Bitcoin

Return: 5%-15%.

If you already possess any Bitcoin, you may earn interest on your assets by lending to other investors or institutions. There are various services that allows you to lend out your Bitcoin in exchange for interest.

However, each network has limitations for loans worth researching. For instance, you might lose part or all of your investment if the borrower you're lending to defaults. Crypto financing is also a relatively new industry and bears a high amount of risk and uncertainty. Notably, numerous sites discontinued providing loan services in 2022. On Nov. 16, 2022, Gemini advised clients they could be unable to withdraw cash from Gemini Earn, and indeed the monies were frozen for users for almost a year.

However, in Feb. 2024, the New York State Department of Financial Services declared that Gemini will repay at least $1.1 billion to consumers who lost money in 2022 .

Accepting payments or tips in Bitcoin

Return: Depends on the quantity of payments in Bitcoin and price fluctuation.

If you take payments or tips for your business or company, consider providing individuals the opportunity to pay in Bitcoin. You can accomplish this using platforms providing processing services like Coinbase or BitPay.

The setup is quite easy; however, understanding the tax consequences and risk involved with taking Bitcoin payments may be more challenging. Coinbase's self-managed account may be set up instantly. BitPay takes a few days to be accepted but enables you to accept multiple coins.

Something to keep in mind: If having exposure to Bitcoin is your objective, make sure to select a provider that enables you to take payments in Bitcoin. While BitPay and Coinbase provide you the option to receive cash this way, other processors only enable you to take transactions in fiat money.

Day-trading Bitcoin Difficulty:

Return: Depends on the amount of investment, transactions and price fluctuations.

It's theoretically conceivable to earn money by buying and selling Bitcoin within short periods, moving in and out of positions as the market fluctuates. But similar to day trading with stocks, it's considerably more probable you will lose money this way.

Stock day traders employ macro- and microeconomic data, market patterns that stretch back to the birth of the stock market, and other resources at their disposal in order to make informed estimates about which stocks to purchase or sell. And nonetheless, these aggressive traders fail to match the gains that may come from purchasing and keeping, say, low-cost funds that follow a wide market index.

Investors have significantly less evidence regarding the behavior of Bitcoin under particular economic situations, therefore forecasting its price swings may be even more challenging. Additionally, trading cryptocurrencies on a daily basis may rapidly become a headache around tax season. You'll need to be vigilant about maintaining records of everything you purchased and sold and the various price points involved. If you're thinking about becoming a regular cryptocurrency trader, it's a good idea to chat with your accountant and make sure you know what to keep track of before getting started.

Some volatility is necessary to make money through day trading; prices need to move up or down for a trader to be able to make a profit. But Bitcoin and crypto are more volatile than other assets, and that makes an already deceptively difficult notion like "buy low and sell high" even more of a challenge. If you're intent on giving this a try, start small and be cautious.

CHAPTER 7

Why Should Entrepreneurs Care About Bitcoin?

Since then, the development of Bitcoin and other cryptocurrencies that expand on the original Bitcoin concept has gone a long way. Although they remain the fundamental application, cryptocurrencies do more than move wealth. Bitcoin and its ecosystem are now mature enough to be depended on for commercial applications.

Is there a benefit to utilizing Bitcoin or other blockchains for your business? This subject is yet unsettled, as many say the influence and ramifications of Bitcoin's technology on business and society are still unclear. Today, the situation with cryptocurrencies is comparable to the condition of development of the World Wide Web 20 years ago. None could predict the social effect of the web across all sectors.

Bitcoin and the underlying blockchain technology were created about a decade ago. It addressed numerous long-standing issues all at once:

- Allowed the transfer of value via the internet without the need to depend on a third party, such as a bank or payment processor
- Created a secure way of payment that can be utilized via the internet without hazards even if the payment address is compromised

- Allowed the storing of value in digital form on the owner's device as opposed to depending on a third party like a bank
- Implemented monetary policies such as the issue of new money and inflation without a central authority
- Incentivized numerous independent actors (miners) to safeguard the network
- Removed single point of failure threats by decentralizing the network
- Created a worldwide currency that operates smoothly across countries
- Implemented pseudonymous payments

Here are 8 ways businesses can use crypto

1. Accept crypto payments

The most apparent choice. You may open your company to worldwide clients by taking Bitcoin and other cryptocurrencies.

There are billions of people in the globe without access to credit or debit cards, and even in the industrialized world, many individuals prefer the security and anonymity of Bitcoin payments. There are various payment processing platforms, and many enable you to change any incoming payments into local fiat currencies quickly if that is necessary for cash flow or account purposes.

Holding Bitcoin is unnecessary if a corporation cares about currency price volatility.

As a merchant, you will gain by avoiding paying the 2-5% credit card and other payment processing costs connected with taking credit card payments. You might even transfer some savings to your consumers to entice additional customers. Credit card payments include downsides, such as longer processing times and higher costs. Credit card transaction fees might dissuade small companies from accepting credit card payments owing to their high cost. Credit card transactions and chargeback fees may also add a considerable financial strain, making Bitcoin a more cost-effective solution. When a chargeback happens, the credit card provider collects the cash from the merchant and adds an extra cost of $5 to $15, which Bitcoin may assist prevent.

As a non-profit, receiving Bitcoin contributions on a static address may bring transparency to your supporters, which is extremely difficult to accomplish with conventional methods.

2. Purchase items and services using Bitcoin

Once you start generating Bitcoin from your clients, you may use Bitcoin to cover your expenditures. You can basically purchase anything online for Bitcoin. You can even pay your phone bills or acquire gift cards for most companies using Bitcoin.

This way, you don't need to worry about conversion costs or credit card security. Suppose you need to make multiple cross-border payments.

In such instance, you may save considerable sums by converting to Bitcoin (assuming your partner allows it) since the cost of Bitcoin transactions is less than a dollar, compared to US$20-30 for a wire transfer or 3-5% for PayPal payments.

Integrating cryptocurrency payments with accounting systems helps speed corporate operations, ensuring that revenue recognition and accounting regulations are implemented similarly to conventional ways. Merchants may assist a crypto transaction via crypto payment systems like BitPay or Coinbase, where users scan a QR code and submit a private key for verification.

3. Use timestamping

The Bitcoin network enables you to immutably record any digitally encoded information at any point.

No one can modify such a timestamp, and it certifies the existence of a specific file or document at that given moment.

Typically, such services are supplied by attorneys, but that is not a mathematically proved technique besides being costly and sluggish.

Suppose you are managing any information that benefits from showing that you have a given piece of information at a certain moment. In that instance, you have a compelling business case for employing timestamping on a blockchain, particularly if you need to do it over the internet and at scale.

4. Run deterministic contracts

Bitcoin, specifically the Ethereum blockchain, can execute reasonably complicated business logic deterministically, mistakenly referred to as "smart contracts."

In reality, this implies that contracts may rely on specific behaviors and perform certain planned actions without human intervention and without the possibility for anybody to modify the rules.

Some triggers in such contracts might be totally automated, such as the passage of time in a retirement contract.

Others must be grounded in real-world occurrences, like an airplane's arrival delay, which a trustworthy individual or organization must disclose to fulfill an insurance contract. Such third-party actors are termed oracles.

As a firm, you may put your business logic inside such a deterministic contract to automate operations, eliminate fraud, and enhance efficiency.

5. Be an oracle

If you read the text above, you know what oracles are.

If you're in a trusted position and have access to particular information that deterministic contract operators may utilize, you can sell your services for a price to give such information.

For example, in the preceding scenario, if you have accurate information on flight arrivals, you may supply such information to an insurance firm that maintains a deterministic contract that pays out when a plane is late for whatever reason.

6. Build goods for the digital currency ecosystem

The crypto ecosystem requires numerous sorts of companies to satisfy the diverse demands of cryptocurrency users, including those dealing with digital currencies.

In addition to cryptocurrency exchanges, numerous digital and hardware wallets, BTMs (Bitcoin ATMs), nodes, security devices, and other specialized services will likely acquire tremendous demand quickly.

Digital money, such as Bitcoin, is a decentralized currency that works independently of conventional financial institutions. Businesses using digital currency must be mindful of the tax ramifications, since the IRS regards Bitcoin as property, mandating thorough record-keeping and accounting to avoid fines.

You may also make and sell items, since the crypto community is enthusiastic.

7. Be a lightning network node

While mining bitcoins may be lucrative, it's incredibly energy-intensive. As a company, you would have to compete with farms adjacent to the cheapest surplus energy sources in the globe.

However, a forthcoming technology will allow for a new form of "mining" of bitcoins. It doesn't take much energy; it only requires a competent computer with a steady internet connection and bitcoins to finance payment channels.

The Lightning Network is a second layer on the Bitcoin network, enabling immediate, confidential, and incredibly inexpensive payments. It is built on nodes that can transport money to other nodes for a minimal cost.

A typical lightning network payment goes via multiple such nodes to reach its destination (called hops), and each node might charge a modest fee to transport such payments.
Currently, the lightning network only consists of a few thousand nodes. Still, it's expanding fast, and we will certainly witness exponential growth once lightning network-enabled wallets enter the app stores.

Nodes that offer multiple channels to services will likely receive tiny fees from millions of payments, amounting to large revenues.
A comparable future business concept is a watchtower. This service monitors the Bitcoin network in real-time and resolves disputes for

lightning network users, even if they are entirely offline. One may charge a modest membership fee to operate such a watchtower.

8. Raise cash using an ICO

ICO is short for Initial Coin Offering. You may represent any real-world or digital asset with tokens created on a blockchain.

You may either develop a clone of Bitcoin (hundreds exist) to generate a new currency representing your asset or leverage an existing blockchain to issue tokens and use those tokens to represent your product.

Then, you may sell those coins or tokens to investors who wish to profit from the increased worth of your tokens.

This effective business strategy garnered hundreds of millions of dollars for organizations who began ICOs despite the possible capital gains taxes involved.

ICOs are regulated in different countries, thus one must carefully follow local legislation. Additionally, companies must understand the tax ramifications of accepting cryptocurrencies, since the IRS views them as property.

Part 3

GETTING STARTED INVESTING IN BITCOIN

CHAPTER 8

How to invest in Bitcoin wisely

Bitcoin is tremendously volatile, but that volatility might generate possibilities for profit if you're trying to trade these digital assets. Cryptos such as Bitcoin and Ethereum have increased a lot since their inception—but they've also endured significant boom-bust cycles along the way. Experienced traders have been speculating on Bitcoin for years, but how do you get started if you're new to the Bitcoin market? Here's how to start investing in Bitcoin and the significant risks you need to watch out for.

5 stages for investing in Bitcoin

First things first, if you're going to invest in Bitcoin, you need to have all your money in order. That involves having an emergency fund in place, a tolerable amount of debt and preferably a diverse portfolio of assets. Your Bitcoin investments may become one more aspect of your portfolio, one that helps boost your overall returns, ideally.

Pay attention to these five additional considerations while you're beginning to invest in cryptocurrency.

1. Take the Time to Understand the Technology

Put aside time to understand the underlying tech powering various crypto assets. Knowing how blockchain networks, consensus methods (e.g., proof-of-work vs. proof-of-stake), hashing algorithms, and smart contracts function can provide you greater insight into a project's potential.

Learning cryptography fundamentals also helps you better appreciate the possibilities of technologies like zero-knowledge proofs. Subscribe to credible industry journals and blogs independent of the crypto you invest in and remain up-to-date on new technical breakthroughs in the area.

So before investing, understand the potential upside and downside. If your financial investment is not backed by an asset or cash flow, it could end up being worth nothing.

2. Use Dollar-Cost Averaging

Use dollar-cost averaging for crypto, which is making tiny, recurrent purchases on a regular schedule, such as weekly or monthly. Automate these purchases via an exchange rather than purchasing manually each time.

Dollar-cost averaging helps you to steadily develop a position while avoiding the psychology of attempting to exactly timing market peaks and bottoms. As a consequence of the tendency of continual price rises, the value of the assets you acquire will grow over time, decreasing the effect of volatility. You might also consider periodically making opportunistic additional purchases when the market declines severely.

3. Manage your risk

If you're trading any asset on a short-term basis, you need to limit your risk, and that may be particularly true with volatile assets such as cryptocurrencies. So as a rookie trader, you'll need to grasp how best to manage risk and build a method that helps you limit losses. And that procedure might differ from person to person:

- Risk management for a long-term investor can simply mean never selling, regardless of the price. The long-term perspective permits the investor to continue with the investment.
- Risk management for a short-term trader, however, can include establishing rigorous guidelines on when to sell, such as when an investment has declined 10 percent. The trader then closely follows the criteria so that a very tiny fall doesn't become a crushing loss later.

Newer traders might consider saving aside a particular amount of trading money and then utilizing just a fraction of it, at least at first. If a position swings against them, they'll still have money in reserve to trade with later. The final point is that you can't trade if you don't have any money. So having some cash in reserve ensures you'll always have a bankroll to finance your trade.

It's vital to limit risk, but that will come at an emotional cost. Selling a lost position sucks, but doing so might help you prevent bigger losses later.

4. Never Invest More Than You Can Afford to Lose

it's vital to avoid placing money that you need into bitcoin. If you can't afford to lose it—all of it—you can't afford to invest it into hazardous assets or any speculative assets, for that matter.

Whether it's a down payment for a home or an essential forthcoming purchase, money that you need in the next few years should be maintained in secure accounts so that it's there when you need it. And if you're seeking an absolutely definite return, your greatest choice is to pay off high-interest debt. You're assured to earn (or save) whatever interest rate you're paying on the loan. You can't lose there.

Finally, don't ignore the security of any exchange or broker you're utilizing. You may control the assets legally, but someone still has to safeguard them, and their security has to be strong. If they don't believe their cryptocurrency is securely protected, some traders prefer to invest in a crypto wallet to retain their coins offline so they're unavailable to hackers or others.

Remember that investing in cryptocurrencies may be part of a bigger investment plan but shouldn't be your only one.

5. Stay Disciplined

Create a strong, rules-based framework. A methodical strategy based on specified criteria helps avoid expensive emotion-driven decision-making. Continually improve your portfolio and approach based on lessons learnt. Remain flexible and receptive to fresh knowledge rather than firmly tying oneself into any one system.

CHAPTER 9

Best Bitcoin Trading Strategies

Bitcoin's volatility presents multiple chances for traders, whether you're searching for short-term gains or long-term value development. Each Bitcoin trading method has its own strengths, adapted to particular timelines, risk tolerances, and market situations. I digs into prominent tactics, including day trading, scalping, swing trading, and HODLing, delivering ideas on how to apply them successfully to Bitcoin's unique market.

Day Trading: Capitalizing on Short-Term Movements

Day trading is purchasing and selling Bitcoin inside a single day, attempting to benefit from modest price swings. This method demands rapid decision-making and access to real-time data to find appropriate entrance and departure spots. For instance, at Bitcoin's peak volatility in 2020, day traders might gain on hourly price changes, entering and leaving bets many times a day. Although successful, day trading takes considerable attention and discipline owing to the ongoing monitoring of market patterns and real-time research.

Swing Trading: Taking Advantage of Price Swings

Swing trading focuses on catching price changes over multiple days or weeks. Unlike day trading, swing traders maintain positions for longer durations, making it suited for people who want a more flexible strategy. Swing traders could initiate Bitcoin positions following a price decline, expecting a comeback over the next week based on technical indicators like moving averages and RSI (Relative Strength Index). This method enables traders to benefit from larger market changes without the need for regular monitoring.

Scalping: Quick Profits in a High-Volume Market

Scalping is an intensive, high-frequency trading method where traders execute several deals in a day, aiming for tiny profits from each trade. Bitcoin's huge trading volumes make it suited for scalpers, who utilize technical analysis and swift execution to exploit minor price swings. For example, scalpers could purchase and sell Bitcoin within minutes when the price swings marginally up or down. Although the individual returns per trade are minimal, scalping may be tremendously successful owing to the number of deals. Scalping demands a thorough grasp of technical analysis and cheap transaction costs.

HODLing: Long-Term Value Investing

HODLing, a phrase coming from a misspelled word for "hold," is a popular technique for long-term investors. HODLers acquire Bitcoin and keep it for years, intending to gain from the asset's general upward direction despite short-term volatility. This approach is suitable to investors who believe in Bitcoin's long-term potential as a store of wealth. For instance, people who purchased Bitcoin in 2015 and kept it earned considerable gains by 2021, despite multiple market declines. HODLing lowers the need for regular market monitoring and transaction expenses, making it excellent for novices and risk-averse investors.

Trend Following: Riding the Market Momentum

Trend following includes detecting and following existing patterns. Traders initiate positions when Bitcoin's price exhibits a clear upward or downward trend, utilizing indicators like moving averages and trendlines to corroborate market direction. For example, traders in early 2021 detected a positive trend as Bitcoin's price soared, initiating long bets and followed the trend until it faded. Trend following involves patience and thorough research, since traders need to wait for trends to completely emerge before committing to positions.

Risk Management: Minimizing Losses and Maximizing Gains

Risk management is crucial to effective Bitcoin trading, particularly owing to the asset's volatility. Traders may minimize possible losses by establishing stop-loss orders, which automatically leave positions at a specified loss level. Position size and risk-reward ratios are also significant since they assist traders calculate the amount of cash to risk on each transaction. Proper risk management ensures that losses are minimized, enabling traders to continue in the market and safeguard their cash over time.

Choosing the proper Bitcoin trading strategy relies on your objectives, risk tolerance, and market knowledge. Whether you favor fast-paced day trading, the flexibility of swing trading, or the long-term approach of HODLing, each method has its own merits. Understanding these methods helps you to implement the strategy that best meets your aims and maximizes your trading results.

CHAPTER 10

Bitcoin and Entrepreneurship

Bitcoin has emerged as a disruptive force in the world of money, and its reach stretches well beyond the boundaries of conventional banks. Entrepreneurs are rapidly understanding the revolutionary potential of cryptocurrencies and blockchain technologies. we will discuss how Bitcoin is transforming entrepreneurship, the potential it brings for businesses, and the hurdles entrepreneurs must negotiate in this fast expanding ecosystem.

1. Unlocking Innovative Fundraising Opportunities:

Bitcoin and blockchain technologies have opened up new channels for businesses to raise funding. Initial Coin Offerings (ICOs) and Security Token Offerings (STOs) have offered entrepreneurs unique financing techniques that circumvent conventional financial institutions.

2. Access to Global Markets:
Bitcoin allows enterprises to access global markets without the need for conventional financial infrastructure. With Bitcoin, cross-border transactions can be conducted rapidly and cost-effectively, giving new potential for corporate development.

3. Empowering Financial Inclusion:
Bitcoin has the ability to empower the unbanked and underbanked communities globally. Entrepreneurs may harness blockchain technology to build financial goods and services

that enable broader access to banking and financial resources.

4. Enhanced Security and Transparency:
Blockchain technology, the backbone of cryptocurrencies like Bitcoin, promises greater security and transparency. Startups may create confidence with customers and investors by providing verifiable and tamper-resistant records of transactions and company operations.

5. Enabling Decentralized Applications (dApps):
Entrepreneurs are embracing blockchain platforms to construct decentralized apps (dApps) that run without a central authority. dApps may disrupt old sectors and redefine business structures, generating new prospects for companies.

6. Navigating Regulatory Complexity:

Bitcoin's decentralized nature has caused regulatory hurdles for companies and investors. Startups must negotiate the expanding legal environment, assuring compliance while driving creativity.

7. Volatility and Risk Management:

The Bitcoin market is notorious for its volatility. Entrepreneurs dealing with cryptocurrencies must carefully handle risks connected with market changes, hedging techniques, and wise financial management.

8. Embracing the Future:

Entrepreneurship and Bitcoin go hand in hand as pioneers embrace the future. Entrepreneurs who adapt to blockchain technology and cryptocurrencies are well-positioned to lead in the digital revolution.

Conclusion

Bitcoin and blockchain technologies are already producing new possibilities and redefining the nature of the corporate environment. For businesses, these technologies make feasible creative and disruptive fundraising approaches, including ICOs and tokenized crowdfunding, an avenue to gather investors from anywhere in the globe, unbounded by physical region. Overall, this democratization of funding helps entrepreneurs finance their firms to expand more effectively and bursting with creativity.

Furthermore, Bitcoin and blockchain enginedeba, thereby decreasing the expenses of a business transaction as well as boosting competitiveness via efficiency in commercial transactions. Global marketplaces are simply available for entrepreneurs to undertake cross border operations without complexity or volatility. These changes make the financial sector more hospitable for previously underbanked or unheard-of people, which, in turn, opens up the latter for sectors where they may become clients.

There is also significant potential for entrepreneurs exploiting blockchain technologies to increase the transparency and security of enterprises. Using blockchain and smart contracts, firms may construct new types of partnerships with customers, partners, and investors, assuring the honesty of the transactions. This trust aspect is extremely significant in creating long-term connections and being able to develop a very strong niche in the market.

Yet, the growth of the Bitcoin ecosystem looks uncertain, and one has to anticipate promptness and adaptability. There is information that has to be retained and followed on technology by the entrepreneurs owing to frequent modifications in certain regulations linked to it in various regions. It would be equally vital for those leading such programs to comprehend these dynamics so as to specify compliance and achieve durable outcomes in the end.

The acceptance of Bitcoin and the larger notion of cryptocurrencies enables start-ups to be some of the first stakeholders in the tech economy of the future. It doesn't stop here, as they can put the heat on and produce enormous improvements across sectors like financial services, supply chain, health, and many more.

Thus, they do not merely capture the rand of today and, at the same time, provide the required circumstances for tomorrow's decentralized and fair economy.

www.ingramcontent.com/pod-product-compliance
Lightning Source LLC
Chambersburg PA
CBHW070347230526
45471CB00006B/2453